Democracy

The Political Saga!

Participative Decision-Making at the Speed of Light

By

Ayele Alemu Teklemariam

Dedicated to my wife of 43 years, Almaz Tesfaye, who has been through it all during our 43 years of marriage and without whom I wouldn't be who I am.

About the Author

A lifelong student of life as it goes through troughs and tumbles, light and darkness and makes a note of his experiences and viewpoints and makes them known by all interested in an effort to make a nano or micro footnote to the totality of human know-how and effort.

Table of Contents

Introduction

A. The author's personal experiences with democracy and dictatorship. B. The influence of these experiences on their perspective on representative democracy II: Democracy vs. dictatorship: A. being expelled from his home country by a dictatorship; B. Being raised in a democratic country: Understanding the contrast between the two systems III Flaws of Representative Democracy: A. Inadequacy in responding to complex and dynamic realities; B. Alienation of elected representatives from the electorate Rule of a minority with low approval ratings IV Advocating for Improvements A. Questioning the Effectiveness of Representative Democracy B. Calling for a more inclusive and transparent decision-making process Need for a system that addresses the challenges of the modern world V. Conclusion A. Recap of the author's personal experiences B. Emphasizing the importance of democracy while acknowledging its shortcomings and urging for improvements in the system to better serve the needs of society Citations: [1] It needs no telling that we have failed to garner consensus on issues of major and minor concern... [2] As development and human civilization have presented us with unprecedented challenges... [3] Now that the great, equally powerful enemy has disappeared from the equation, intra-party squabbles... [4] The implements and gadgets of modern life are more and more dependent on parts and physical realities... [5] Back then, my birth country had a powerful ally, and my adopted country had a powerful enemy...

Democracy and Dictatorship

From the outset, I recognize that if I make an effort to define or express both or one of the terms in the heading, I would be doing a disservice to all who have debated and done millennia's worth of work and effort that I dare not. Yet it goes without saying that I may add a micro or nano footnote to the discourse conducted, research done, and efforts made to date by my mere existence and having a taste of them both by first having experienced and second and third having learned.

Talking about first-hand experiences, one had thrown me out of my country of birth, and the other had taken me with open arms and raised me as one of its own adapted.

When you claim first-hand experience, there can be no substitute for taste, comparison, and contrast, and often, being able to see the world from two perspectives is far superior to seeing it from only one, as you can truly understand what the other feels only by putting yourself in his shoes or being him and backing yourself. Back then, my birth country had a powerful ally, and my adopted country had a powerful enemy that shaped their souls and physical beings. When they both lost that friend and enemy, they seemed to be losing their souls and their essence, their sense of security, and their confidence, making me wonder whether having a strong enemy wasn't as bad as I thought it was, for it will force you to stand well anchored, priorities well sorted out, and trivialities set aside. When the power of your enemy is such that you or the enemy can annihilate the other with the push of a button, there could, of course, be no time for gimmicks; there could only be serious business, and that was how we all remembered it.

On matters of vital national and international interests that affected all or most citizens, often a broad consensus and agreement that transcended ideological and party lines were sought and achieved, and those differences were considered and thought about as luxuries that could be lived without until all was fine and collective national security and national interests were met and secured. Often, those ideas deeply held by the far right and left swung in and out of favor as the elections were won and lost by opposing parties. In effect, the presence of that powerful enemy acted as a fourth check in addition to the three balances of our three-branched system of government to seek a broad consensus on matters of governance and policy, be they national or international. It kept interparty and ideological disputes as secondary disputes for discussion, voting, and agreement. Now that a great, equally powerful enemy has disappeared from the equation, intraparty squabbles have come to the foreground as primary conflicts and a one- and two-vote majority dictatorship has become the norm as if democracy meant a dictatorship of or by the majority, the very thought and possibility the founding fathers worked so hard to prevent from happening in their deliberations on the formulation of the states.

Democracy (western liberal democracy, that is) has its differences from any other form, for there are many variations of it. It was supposedly a system where actions and decisions were made based on broad consensus while issues of contention were to be debated, examined, and researched until a broad consensus was reached and not dictated by a simple or even considerable majority. If that were the case, we would have long fallen into the abyss of history before we knew it. Why is reaching a consensus harder now than then? In modern society, reaching a consensus has become increasingly challenging due to various factors. One significant factor is the prevalence of absolute relativism, which has led to fragmented realities and subjective interpretations of truth. Additionally, the emphasis on individual uniqueness and the primacy of the individual has created a tension between individualism and the need for a nurturing social environment.

The rapid advancement of technology and globalization has also contributed to the divergence of interests and the divergence of global perspectives, making consensus more difficult to achieve.

The Lessons of Brit-Exit

The era of collective security and collective well-being that started right after the end of the First World War and failed to guarantee collective security was followed by the Second World War, in whose aftermath the United Nations and the continental unions were born, which were epitomized by the European Union after the end of the Cold War. The European Union, with all the pitfalls and turmoil, ups and downs, and tangible success stories, at least for a while, seems like an experiment in the future of humanity living in socioeconomic and culturally defined boundaries that are otherwise bounded only by natural barriers, the natural boundaries that defined continents. At least for a short while, humanity seemed to be moving in the direction of free movement, free trade, and free choice of domicile.

The individual seemed on the move to where he would be a free agent to sell his labor to whoever was willing to pay him, despite the small locality he was born and raised in. What mattered was that his ability and uniqueness endowed him with talent that fit his needs. Talent and skills seemed on the march to meet fine and refined demands and needs on a wider and broader scale, enabling unexploited human capabilities that benefited and could benefit all of humanity on a bigger and wider scale that would otherwise remain in the dark in the dark corners of a bounded this or that territory. Small and frail local and national businesses get the continental and beyond exposures, reaping better and bigger returns on their labor, both intellectual and physical. While

cyber-global citizenship has already been ushered in with the advent of the internet and all the rest of the virtues of the cyber-world, the physical world has remained a drag on this fast-moving reality. At one point, the collusion of these two realities would have been expected, and perhaps that manifested itself in some ways in the British exit movement, the poll, and the result. It is my understanding that the 2016 Brit exit movement and vote result will generate volumes of work in the years to come by academics, politicians, journalists, and others, as what has already been generated indicates, for it is a reversal in a movement and a trajectory and mindset with broader lasting effects not limited to the UK and Europe but to the world at large. The fact that on the opposite side of the Atlantic, an America first campaign is wedged in the format and content makes it already of global importance and significance, and if another like victory is achieved, the possible transatlantic alliances makes the significance even larger by that much, which makes a thorough understanding if possible and a reasonable grasp at the least to turn around the mirror and look what we all look like inside it is profoundly important. The Brit Exeter's campaign was wedged on the fear of the unknown, the "unknown" that is known enough that the whole world, including the British themselves, can positively testify that this unknown is not known for anything but for having done the world overwhelmingly well with minimal proper handling.

This unknown is the immigrant next door and the one at the border who is looking yet to come in. Yes, there are monsters among them as there are among us; there could possibly be psychopaths among them as there are among us; and all the ills of humanity that pervade among us do amongst them, but these are all fears that we carry with them in or with them out. Like all adventures of human endeavors and ventures, there are payments to be made and prizes to be gained, and there are some who understand exactly that those immigrants, or the overwhelming majority of them, are not coming to eat from anyone's plate but coming to the table with their own plates given the proper handling and the opportunity, and that has been proven time and again. This would have been the one fundamental truth that is not as hidden as it looks and would and should have eased the anxiety of the Brits' but didn't. Why?

Looking at what has been said and done during the campaign prior to the campaign and post-campaign, the simplicities and plainness of the rhetoric are appealing, as all simplicities are, but almost everything in nature and nature itself is intricate, complex, and intertwined. It is revealing to read some of the statistics of the poll and results to uncover some of the complex interplays of some of the moving parts and wonder if there is a comparative relevance here. People often pay special attention to matters of the pocket even more than matters of the heart, and we are all living testaments to that. The warning and repeated appeal by the overwhelming majority of British economists, academics, forums, opinion makers, polls, and pundits that the exit will for sure pinch them in their pockets simply fell on deaf ears in unprecedented defiance of professional opinion and professionalism itself.

Perhaps this is telling that professional opinion, more than at any time in history, is considered a commodity that is bought and sold by the highest bidder in an auction house (media), that it is worth the money paid to the buyer and is not to be taken at face value. The thrust between the professional as expressed in the media and the common man, or nonprofessional, is breached, and professionalism is a collateral victim as vulgar, raw, barbaric self-expressions and expressions of others in the mainstream media are taken as acceptable fads as though refinements and edge smoothings are not the trademarks of civilization. It is a pity to see professionalism injured in such a way and to such a degree, though the wound is partially self-inflicted.

Age matters, to use the fad and jargon of the time. In a poll on June 23, 2016, when people aged 60 and over forced an exit vote majority, 70% of the people aged 18 to 24 voted remain. It is obvious that age matters. Traditionally, at the times when traditional family and transgenerational relations were made, people rarely reached the age of 60, let alone lived past it. Today, 60 is just the beginning of yet another 30 or 20 years ahead, perhaps even more in the coming years. Then a person of 60 will have not too many years to deal with a 30-year-old in common that he cares less for himself as to what happens tomorrow or after that was the worry left for and by 30 years, and theirs was a worry for them than themselves. Today, 20 or 30 years into the future, is not simply for 30-year-olds. The Grady's and Granny's are here to share it and are claiming the stakes are as high for them, and that is clearly demonstrated by the Brit-exciter's overwhelming vote to exit. Yet, in some ways, the conflict seems to be a conflict between a world and wealth made yesterday and a commonwealth world to be made tomorrow. By all measures, tomorrow favors the young over the grannies and grandees, and in whatever tomorrow brings, their share is limited or is a minority for the foreseeable future. The preservation of the pi that was made in the confinements and bounds of yesterday and the desire to make a pi of tomorrow in the unbounded large-scale free space of tomorrow, the optimism and hope of the times to come, and the nostalgia and past glory of the world gone by are at odds, and demographics and depth of pocket were at work and had shown who is yet in control.

The advent of social media, the availability and proliferation of knowledge via digital media deprived professionals of the value of professional skill and authority in matters of professions and authoritative referenceable truth around which contending parties and thought trends could coalesce. Knowledge, skill, and authority became fully commoditized, where the best could be sold and bought for the best money, rendering truth to be a victim of money and a reality of the beholder.

Furthermore, the behavior of government officers has evolved, leading to a shift in the checks and balances of the system. The loss of a common global compass in world democracies has allowed territorial strongmen to rise, further hindering the consensus-building process. These factors, along with the complexities and intricacies of modern life, have made it challenging to establish a shared understanding and reference point for consensus. The emergence of multinationals whose interests and allegiances transcend national and other forms of group belongings with annual and monthly budgets far superior to those of many mid-level countries, with their interests represented at all levels of government, makes the interests of the public and the private, the interests of the corporation, and the state often to collide or be at odds for reaching a reasonable consensus.

Rituals and rites have long been important in forming political structures and preserving social order in communities all over the world. Through these actions, social cohesion was strengthened, authority structures solidified, and legitimacy was bestowed. But occasionally, the rite of passage can also become a source of unrest since it can reveal and subvert established power structures, which can result in changes to society or even uprisings. Rituals and rites are frequently used by leaders to demonstrate their legitimacy and win the people's trust by serving as a symbolic display of power and authority. By taking part in these rituals, people support the stability of society as a whole and reaffirm their loyalty to the established power structures. However, when particular people or groups of people feel excluded or marginalized by these customs, it fuels discontent and social unrest, which in turn leads to significant changes in society. During these turbulent times, through the mechanisms of rituals, rites, and rites of passage, marginalized voices have had the chance to question the status quo. Rites of passage and rituals are insuperable, as a ceremony without the proper rituals is tantamount to no ceremony at all. A general without his uniform and a judge without his robe automatically lose their prestige at the location and fail to command the respect and authority that come with their respective roles. Similarly, without established rituals and traditions, important events and milestones in society may lose their significance and fail to bring people together in a meaningful way. Rituals are mechanisms by which people are assigned codes of conduct and attributes to their proper specialties and are expected to act according to prescribed written or unwritten forms and formalities of a community. Partial or total disregard for the proper rituals and conduct of the community deprives members of the community of a means and way of reaching a consensus on matters of importance and significance. Rites of passage are ceremonies to accept new members of a class of people who have fulfilled all the requirements that will entitle an individual or group of individuals to the privileges and status enjoyed and entertained by the accepting group.

As such, school graduations on all levels, marriages, baptisms, coronations, and inaugurations are all investitures conferred on individuals who could have been commoners or ordinary prior to the observances of the rites. Ascendence to position and status, credence, authority, and legitimacy could only be achieved and entertained after having gone through the rites of passage. In contrast to modern liberal democracy's assertion that legitimacy to power only emanates from a democratic plebiscite, political, social, professional, and religious legitimacy has and still emanates from proper conduct, rites, rituals, and rites of passage, the often taken for granted notion of the source of legitimacy, particularly that of political legitimacy, maybe a notion whose time has come and passed, as is indicated by many societies' all over.

In exploring potential solutions to human progress and technological and scientific advancement, the role of blockchain technology may be one of many possibilities that could help change the status quo in promoting democracy and social justice. However, there are concerns expressed about the implementation of on-chain governance, arguing for capable technologists to govern blockchains rather than relying solely on democratic processes. It is significant to highlight the importance of transparency, accountability, and the direct, real-time participation of every electorate in decision-making processes, as is the case in blockchains. In conclusion, while reaching a consensus in modern society is difficult, there are opportunities for improvement through technological advancements and reevaluating governance systems. By addressing the factors that hinder consensus-building and promoting transparency and accountability, it may be possible to overcome these challenges and foster a more inclusive and participatory decision-making process. Now the fourth check on the behavior and acts of our government has somehow morphed, changed, or disappeared altogether. The behavior of our officers in government had evolved and acquired behaviors that would have been inconceivable then, such as the interdependence of nature's beings, an act of one causing a chain of other surprising and expected happenstances and physical realities. Implements and gadgets of modern life are more and more dependent on parts and physical realities that are delicate, minute, and infinitesimal in size and complex in their interactions and relationships that are susceptible to infinitesimal changes for colossal effects and aftereffects. What civilization has brought to the modern way of life is a level of complexity unprecedented in history and continues. We are living in a time when and where life-changing information flies from one corner of the globe to the other at the speed of light, necessitating decision-making and consensus-building capabilities on the fly and instantaneously.

Off all things known, time has become the most valuable commodity, and ever more so with every passing fraction of it. These and others, more or less closely associated and interactive with these phenomena, are what render the hitherto existing representative democracy inept and none agile enough to appropriately and in time respond to the highly dynamic social, economic, and political realities of today's and tomorrow's world. This truth has been and is being evidenced by the continued alienation of the elected representatives from the electorate, where the elected are ruling with unprecedented negative approval ratings as though they were put to power by some aliens. And the funny thing is that this is not even a one- or two-nation phenomenon but a global one. When the elected rules with the approval of a small minority of the electorate and not with a broad majority consensus, you call it by any name, but to me, it is a dictatorship of a minority. It matters little or not at all that one is elected by a majority. One is not judged only by how it began or ended, but rather by one's whole life, end to beginning, and by the measures of the value of modern-day life, which is a whole lot of time for anyone and anything. Four years and two years of plebiscites and two and four-year ballets are eternities to be considered participation in the affairs and matters of nations' affairs that change drastically in matters of nanoseconds and microseconds that affect the livelihood of every citizen in ways one will have a hard time recognizing oneself after the decisions are made. I feel it would serve as a great example of what I call "Morsi syndrome ". The Egyptian President, Mohammed Morsi, was a democratically elected president for four years until he declared he would do as he wished for the four years and would not seek or want popular support during his term. In his efforts to dictate his way through his term, he ended his reign with an uprising that toppled him from office.

That syndrome seems somehow widespread and rubbed off despite the degree of affliction and prevailing barriers to its rampant manifestations, even in some of the full-fledged Western democracies like ours. As development and human civilization have presented us with unprecedented challenges of complexities and intricacies, the challenges have never passed unmet at any time in the past, nor are they being unmet now or will they be in the future. There are tale-tale signs we are on the verge of creating and developing technological and scientific capabilities that will enable perhaps societies of today, but surely of the future, that participation of every electorate on every measure and decision made and be directly accountable and that every decision made by known and transparently made and every electorate be enabled and spared from the frustrations of the acts and decisions made for him by his representatives and be left with the only recourse available to him to reward or punish his representative long after the measure has been passed, his money and time spent beyond recovery and he would have a hard time remembering what he was like before those decisions were made on his behave.

It was such a per suit that had such a romantic Puritan sense and purpose, finding out the truth about, the how, and when of things and a delight in one's knowledge. A knowledge unknown before that is about to be revealed to one, and the when why, and how of it all that used to be what drives the academic, the intellectual, and the researcher, though their discoveries and their revelations that led to the making of life better in many, large, few, and small ways and perhaps the creation of wealth thereof, fame, and prestige for some and all, the principals were used to doing it just for the pleasure of knowing, even when their pursuit of knowledge led to the discovery of ugliness hidden, a misery and dread unknown or caused where there were none before. It is often uncertain where and what one's pursuit of discovery might turn up: ugly, beautiful, easy, or difficult; nevertheless, the thrill of knowing remained and presenting just as it is to all used to have such a sense of duty and responsibility to humanity, unlike today, where it could possibly be doctored and customized to fit the needs of a higher bidder in the market place and sold.

It is the age of cosmetic surgery, where even the rough edges of the human face are rounded and smoothened to fit a known stereotype. Yes, knowledge has always been used to smooth the rough edges of reality to fit our purpose, and it will continue to do exactly that, except that everybody knew what it was like before it went under cosmetic surgery to smoothen the edges and knew where and which edges were smoothened. Before we are done lamenting about the age of physical alteration, fashion, and cosmetics, we are confronted with the age of genetic engineering, whereby our core fundamentals are manipulable to the desires of ourselves and perhaps our parents and society at large. Whereas the foundational specifics and common programs that made us and could possibly enhance or diminish us, fundamental specific and common genetic programming bugs that make us twitch and turn in certain pre-configured formats can and are sent across the globe and beyond at the speed of light, our decision-making process is perhaps is not only lagging but stagnant. All through such dynamic scientific, social, and technological transformations, the one thing that remained permanent and led us to believe that it had served us well until the reality of it hit us right in the face was our system of democratic representative democracy, which has remained in large measures intact since its formulation in the age of the horse buggy. Venter, J. C.

I am not by any means suggesting that all this time it has not been subjected to face lifts, cosmetics, minor and major surgeries to round off some rough edges, mend some broken bones, or get dressed with the fashions of the times; I am just saying it hasn't been catching up with not only changing times but accelerating changes. As we are told convincingly by scientists, our universe, and perhaps all universes if there are many, are expanding at an accelerated rate. If that is the case, I have no reason to suspect it. Otherwise, some of our progress is on par with and is being followed at the same pace while others are lagging behind, and if the lag continues, they might not survive the forces that are pulling forward by any amount of futile backward drag. It needs no telling that we have failed to garner consensus on issues of major and minor concern when we speak of our state of democracy, not here or there, but everywhere.

When some have retained and been entertained by a pinhole view of the world, others have developed a 360-degree view of the world, and the gap is that wide and narrow in many aspects of our modern-day lives. While parts of our society are living and conducting their daily lives in a boundless cyberspace figuratively and literally, and their interests and loyalty transcend the long-established norms and bounds and encompass a much larger entity than it was like years ago, part of our communities have narrowed and bounded interests and loyalties even more than we had entertained a few years ago. These are viewpoints and interests that are as odd as they could ever be. As these forces are tearing our reality in two opposite directions, we seem to have lost our consensus-based global compass that guided the world democracies in a unified direction, giving rise to the prominence of local and territorially strong men who do as they see fit over their dominions. Territorial dominions, economic dominions, cultural dominions, etc., got fortified, controlled, and dominated by strong men devoid of traditional community rules, rites and rituals and proper conduct, which led to the creation of technology and a flight by many who lost confidence and thrust on the world ruled and controlled by dispersed territorial strong men to the unbounded, enabling, private, and yet public new cyber world of the crypto blockchain's. Perhaps it is worth it to say a few words and consider as well what has thus far been said about the crypto-blockchains prior to discussing their democratic nature, applications to help promote democracy and social justice attributes. As this technology just sprang into the technology scene, it is already branching, morphing, and fast mutating into varied species of its own, and it is just beginning.

"I assert that it is not just Bitcoin's proof-of-work wasted computation on crypto-cracking that is the problem. Don't get me wrong, Bitcoin multiplies the problem a thousandfold, but the fundamental problem remains. Bitcoin burns more electricity than the whole country of Ireland to achieve about five transactions per second. That is a pitiful and unforgivable waste." Arthur Brock:

I understand the concerns of the notable gentleman, yet what seems to have been forgotten here is that Bitcoin was the pioneer, and like many pioneering technologies riddled with inefficiencies, inefficiencies are, by the way, innate in all pioneering technologies and nature itself, but a work in progress otherwise evolution and progress would holt. It would only take one to see how efficient our pioneering 19th-century technologies were to see the mounds left behind and the mountains removed for and from the coal mines of yesteryear and see how far those technologies have come. Is it any wonder that blockchain technology has progressed by bits and bounds as we speak and continues at unprecedented speed, forcing us to admit that, indeed, the universe is expanding and time is running faster as a result?

"Take 7,000 people (the approximate number of current bitcoin "miners"). Have each person fill out a ballot for whoever they think should be the next President of the U.S. Then have them each take a clear box with 20 dice in it. The first one to be able to shake their box and get all 20 dice to land as ONES gets to have their ballot be the only one that counts as long as everyone else agrees the candidate's name was spelled correctly and meets the legal criteria (over 35 years old and a natural-born citizen). Would any normal human call that an election by "consensus?"" Arthur Brock:

Yes! Rolling dies and coming up with whatever preconceived result may be nonsensical, yet the reality of that nonsensical result is determined by consensus and the fact that with the nonsensical process, that nonsensical result was reached by consensus seems evident. To me, consensus is not about the process or the result of the process but about whether that result was reached by being voted on and determined that nonsense is indeed nonsense. The greatest take here is not how Bitcoin is created by a nonsensical, wasteful process but that consensus can indeed be reached about any reality at all with the participation of every member of the blockchain chain and that the decision of everyone is immutable and acknowledged. As to the problem to solve, the world is awash with problems, and humanity can use its brain and computing power to solve any problem as long as it is incentivized, recognized, and credited properly and dully. Dowelling on the nonsensical ways and nonsensical results of BitCoin may be unnecessary. By the way, there is no other like nature that plays rolling dies in its solutions to all its ways; nature never had a blueprint from which it refers its actions; it just does it by chance and necessity, whether dies are rolled or not.

"This is wrong. Data does not have some kind of independent existence. It is always asserted by some agent (a device, sensor, person, or process). To divorce data from its provenance and behave like it is an existential or ontological entity is a fundamental misclassification. It is not a rock sitting on the road. In fact, many people now understand that rock does not have some fundamental "is" - ness. There are a multitude of possible states—quantum probabilities that only resolve through an interaction. Well... This is even more important for data in decentralized systems. To optimize these systems for unaccountable anonymity and structure them for random "consensus" is to destroy the integrity and provenance of data." Arthur Brock:

Yes, one cannot expect either data or reality to be absolute and static; the sciences of relativity, calculus, and mathematical statistics come to the rescue and say everything is relative and dynamic, and nothing is exact, but at a most possible approximation, and the approximations continue to improve in time as we work to improve and stumble upon better ways. "Do you think there's a reason why each cell in your body just manages its own state rather than synchronizing with some global cell ledger?" Arthur Brock.

Yes, there is, and yes, they do. As I have said earlier, it is true that inefficiencies are common in nature. Perhaps that proves more than anything that life is a product of a longtime trial and error experiment that is inefficient, prone to mistakes, and able to learn from and correct mistakes and move on. Above all, in its effort not to forget its progress, demise, failure, departure, and confluence, it made it its duty to archive it in its DNA. Life in its DNA does not only carry its operating daily program but the whole archive of its history from eons past. If that were not true, how would we be able to find out the identity of someone from a single drop of blood, a single hair sample, or from any bodily fluid left at a scene? Or ponder about our ancestry and heritage. To answer the author's question, yes, each cell in any living organism carries an identical copy of the same DNA sequence despite the state of expression of particular genes at a particular cell function, and if, by any chance, an alien cell gets introduced anywhere in the system, as is clear from elementary biology, it will be attacked by specialized cells and killed. Yes, it is redundant, but perhaps for a reason not to give a chance to mistakes and rout them out if they arise, and yes, such a mistake or unexpectedly arising and survived scenarios have, in turn, gone on creating or forming if you wish redundant copies carried on by all members of the site's system yet again to retain the newly formed statuesque. I am sure knowledgeable people could write pages on the issue, but it would suffice to say that much from my layperson to point out the fallacy I thought was of the argument iterated nonetheless.

"Yet... The "consensus" process described above exists precisely to manufacture the official timeline by which everything happened. If we both tried to spend a Bitcoin token at "the same time," different nodes would each receive our transactions in different orders and would have to reject whichever one they received second. Then the lottery of hash-cracking begins and eventually selects a node's vantage point as the official universal timeline." Arthur Brock.

Exactness, I am sure the author knows, is an illusion we are willing to entertain while we all know it is nonexistent in the real sense of the word. Precision is merely dependent on possible only on measurable and knowable quantities by direct and indirect means available at a time in a place and at no time and place in the past or present had all those quantities been fulfilled nor will they be in the future denying us of our desire and need to be exact, unfortunately, we have to settle for the best possible, and that well has been, that is and will always be the way. The great discovery of Sir Isaac Newton's, the science of calculus, for which precision mathematics is praised and celebrated, acknowledges and dowels on its limitation of the theory of limits of that dreadful "delta" approaching zero but never zero. Take that approximation out of the equation, and the whole fabric of calculus crumbles into pieces, and the implications are far-reaching. Perhaps that is why, as well, Feynman concluded that there is ample at the bottom because, in his effort to reach the bottom, he must have hit this bottomless bottom as

Epsilon approaches and never approaches what it ought to approach. It has been long established that there is no such thing as a universal time, universal rest, or universal speed, but if I am not mistaken, and I stand corrected if I am, it is often possible to establish a common reference time and a common reference speed. As such, the speed of light serves as a common reference to which all other speeds could be referenced, to be precise enough, at least for practical purposes. Isn't the issue here to establish a reference time from which every other time is measured and not establish a universal time? If there is only such an animal? And how else would that reference be established if not by consensus? Don't get me wrong, I am not by any means defending or standing for the inefficiency of Bitcoin's ways or any other, but merely trying to point out that the criticisms leveled against it being not compatible with the ways of nature may be somewhat skewed or are flawed, if not fully. Perhaps my layman's opinion of Arthur Brock's take on Bitcoin's ways is said more than enough that I would turn my attention and the reader's, if any, to the presumed or thought of the blockchain technology's aspect of contribution to democracy and equality of humanity and the misperceptions thereof as my layman has been able to see it.

Unlike a drop of water that loses its identity when it joins the ocean, man does not lose his being in the society in which he lives. Man's life is independent. He is born not for the development of the society alone but for the development of himself. " Self-sovereign identity is a scarcely developed resource, accessible only to a tech-savvy few in mostly developed countries. With the advent of blockchain technology and its application to identity management through projects like Civic and uPort, the layman's ability to exclusively maintain her own data is gradually becoming a reality. But, in developing countries, a whole host of infrastructural and geo-political problems prevent a massive market of 'identity-non-consumers" from freely transacting and exchanging their identity and associated attributes in any context they see fit." Robert Greenfield IV:

If my layperson has a fascination and wonderment about this new movement and discovery and technological discovery, what needs to be said is the very possibility of self-sovereign identity and immutability of data and that identity surpasses all others by any measure. As all new and old discoveries and revelations come with their own challenges to overcome and never overcome, self-sovereignty's challenges may be two-pronged: escaping the control of a central issuing authority and the loss of the immutability of self-issued sovereign identity. Perhaps identity begins at a time when an individual applies or enrolls as whichever term best applies to the blockchain and gets approval or acceptance. If that is the case, one can often clear-wash whatever predates the date of one's assignment of identity. If, on the other hand, one is to get registered at birth and issued an identity, wonder if that does not infringe on the so-called sovereignty unless otherwise claimed that real sovereignty starts at an age when one is endowed with privileges and burdened with responsibility. In a consensus-based blockchain system, the greatest beauty is that everything is known, and everybody is anonymous. Every member knows every member's activities, as they are all approved and disapproved by consensus, and nobody knows anybody unless there arises a need, and only with consent or coercion if there is a compelling reason for the individual to be identified.

As indicated in the quote above, a person is both a society and an individual identity, not an individual self-contained and self-sufficient all in one entity nonetheless, that is endowed with rights, privileges, and responsibilities whereby a degree of sovereignty will be infringed upon out of the need to hold the individual responsible and accountable to make sure that dues are made payable for the privileges entertained. It is only a short time memory that the offshore banking of yesteryears served as the blockchains and sovereign identities of yesteryears that served some segments of societies all over the world to avoid responsibilities while enjoying the maximum privileges their respective societies offered until the famously known Panama Papers revealed the unpaid dues and responsibilities hidden in the glittering Panama City and the Caiman Island skyscrapers. That, I suppose, is what happens when "man's life is independent. He is born not for the development of society alone, but for the development of himself." without paying his dues. The social and political decadence that seems to be the solution and most of the ills of decadent liberal democracy and the mafia-style dictatorship of the oligarchy of newly out of communist and socialist convert societies and politics suffer from may be remedied to an extent by this infant new consensus-based crypto-anonymous identity, fully transparent activity, and immutable data blockchain technology. The mere fact that in a consensus-based blockchain, for the reality of an activity to be acknowledged in time, it had to be reached by a 50+1-member majority of the membership of the blockchain is transparent to all members of the blockchain and can't be altered makes it hard or impossible to make a move or act in ways that compromise what an officially accepted norm, convention, legal, and ethical standard without being flagged and known by all is. Every act of every self-sovereign identity is put under the microscope, for it had to be validated by the majority of the membership and propagated to the whole community, which had a vested interest in what, when, and how of its community and if it becomes a must and action necessary in who. The other additional beauty of the technology is that all data generated by all members reside everywhere on the chain and can't be deleted from one local or central datastore, though it can be edited by the authorized or owner, yet the new version coexists with the previous version or versions and can't be overwritten or white-outed, which perhaps will save us from the likes of arguments, waste of time, energy, and money over lost emails or other documents that plagued the last campaign of the Democratic Party.

Perhaps I am too optimistic, or perhaps even overoptimistic, yet an aspect of human life is very much being experimented with and proven to be working, and I would like to believe that when a technology is proven to be working in solving one narrow specialized aspect of human need, it won't be long before it is adopted to solve other challenges of humanity, such as the cell phone, which was a mere voice communication tool before it became literally and figuratively the brain extensions that we can't last a minute separated from it.

Blockchains should not be democracies. How do you govern a blockchain? That might sound like a strange question. In theory, blockchains aren't supposed to be governed at all—they're supposed to be "permissionless decentralized ledgers. But a blockchain is more than just a ledger. It's also an ecosystem of software, an economy of merchants, companies, and exchanges, and beneath all that, a community of developers, miners, and users. At the end of the day, blockchains must live in the messy world of humans and their quarrels. Otherwise, the data on its ledger would hold no sway in the real world. There are many important decisions to make in how a blockchain evolves. And so, blockchains must be governed. Their governors are inevitably humans. The only question is: which humans, and how are those humans' decisions enforced? Approaches to blockchain governance in broad strokes, there are two approaches to governing a blockchain. The first approach is off-chain governance. This is basically the way most private institutions are governed—individuals who are trusted by the community come together and form a group which is responsible for blockchain's governance and well-being. That group is tasked with fixing bugs and security vulnerabilities, adding features and improving scalability, representing the blockchain in public discussions, and maintaining the right balance of power among users, companies, and miners. At a glance, this looks quite centralized. But there's always the potential for mutiny. If enough users disagree with the protocol governance, they can initiate a hard fork and create a parallel blockchain, which is exactly what happened with Bitcoin Cash and Ethereum Classic. The threat of forking is a powerful check against poor governance by the core team. Most of the major blockchains are governed by a soft governance process like this. Bitcoin, Ethereum, Litecoin, Monero, and ZCash all follow this model. But there is a second type of governance model that's gaining steam, known as on-chain governance. On-chain governance rejects the centralization inherent in the off-chain model. In on-chain governance models, users within the blockchain directly vote on decisions to be made. Depending on how the vote turns out, the blockchain automatically enforces the outcome of that vote. This all happens intra-protocol. On-chain governance is central to many "blockchain 3.0" projects, such as Tezos, DFINITY, and Cosmos. Others, such as 0x and Maker, are planning to eventually implement on-chain governance through a more gradual transition. On-chain governance is a radical proposition. It attempts to sidestep the messy human dramas of traditional organizations. Instead, it wants to turn a blockchain into a self-governing, mechanistic democracy. Just as Bitcoin allowed users to have sovereignty over their money, on-chain governance would allow users to govern their entire financial system. It echoes the tantalizing idealism of the Enlightenment and the French Revolution. As an abstract idea, it sounds grand. But on-chain governance is dangerous, and I worry it will lead to disastrous outcomes. Blockchains should not be democracies, and the reasons why are subtle and counterintuitive. On the blockchain, no one knows who you are. Democracies operate under the principle of "one person, one vote." But blockchains are pseudonymous—you are only known by your cryptographic keys. This means anyone can trivially create a new identity by generating a new set of keys. This poses a problem: to create a democracy on the blockchain, you'd need to solve the Sybil problem, which means you need to know everyone's real-world identity. This would require a globally trusted identity broker. So far, no such broker exists, and it's hard to imagine such a thing being created any time soon. So, given that we have no global identity system, on-chain governance schemes don't actually try to enforce a one-person, one-vote rule. Instead, they implement a "one-coin, one-vote" rule via proof of stake. This is intended to be a loose proxy for democracy since coins are scarce and cannot be trivially generated. But the proof of stake implies that those with more coins have proportionally more weight in their votes. This is explicitly not a democracy—at best, it's a plutocracy. Maybe this is okay. You could argue it forces voters to have more skin in the game, and perhaps large coin holders should have more say in protocol governance since they have more to lose. On the other hand, you could make the same argument that large corporations should have more influence over government legislation—they have more at stake financially than the average citizen, so shouldn't corporations have more legislative control? It's obvious that this argument misses something important. Plutocracy explicitly privileges the financially powerful and lets them exploit those with fewer resources. But what's the alternative? A bunch of dudes on a development team making all the important decisions? What government has ever been run by a bunch of developers? Don't confuse blockchains with nations. Let's sidestep the plutocracy question and pretend that "one coin, one vote" is an effective proxy for democracy. I'll grant that democracy is a fantastic system for governing a nation. But blockchains are not nations, and most governance is not democratic. Businesses are not democracies; militaries are not democracies; nonprofits are not democracies and open-source software projects are not democracies. There are good reasons for this. Remember, blockchains are, first and foremost, experimental software. They are evolving rapidly and have many unresolved technical challenges. For example, Ethereum's roadmap involves transitioning its consensus protocol to proof of stake, completely rewriting its virtual machine, and implementing a sharding scheme, and there's a bunch more in between. This is hard, technical stuff. It's more akin to administrating CERN than administrating a country. We have good models for how to govern hard, technical projects; they look like the Linux Foundation or the IETF. They don't look like democratic institutions led by the masses. A good technology governance process should be built around the expertise of capable technologists who can balance technical robustness against practical concerns. They should plan out and deliver on technical roadmaps. In short, they should get shit done. Democracies do the opposite. They campaign, they propagandize, they filibuster, they divide themselves into parties, and they steer away from risks. In this system, anything without consensus is discarded, and enormous energy is expended, convincing the average voter on some point of policy or another. Don't get me wrong: despite all the friction, democracy is the right kind of process for governing a nation-state! But it is definitely the wrong model for governing an experimental technology. Let's be honest. This stuff is still very early. I don't want my grandmother even using the blockchain right now, and I definitely don't want her voting on protocol upgrades. But there's a second reason why the analogy between blockchains and nations is broken: you can always exit a blockchain. Freedom, Forks, and Exit: Exiting a country is hard. Even if you don't like the way your country is governed, you may not necessarily have the resources to emigrate. Even if you do, the government may not let you leave, and neighboring countries might not be hospitable. One doesn't choose one's birthplace. There's some coercion inherent in simply being born. Thus, you could argue that a country is bound to protect the welfare of its citizens since those citizens can't always vote with their feet. Blockchains are different. If you don't like your blockchain's choices, you can sell your coins and migrate to a different blockchain. Better yet, you can drum up support for a fork—or, if you're enterprising enough, manage a new fork yourself, as several groups have done to Bitcoin in the last year. To be clear, forking is not free. But relative to emigrating from a country, it's pretty cheap. In an ecosystem where everyone can vote with their wallet, it's not clear that democracy buys you that much as a governance model. "Qureshi Follows Entrepreneur."

Crypto.

As it is clear from the above long quotation, it is long because I found it hard to leave a part of it and make a relevant and contextually valid argument or reference to it, and I found the author's opinion to be that of a person of authority, which is noteworthy and must be read in its entirety. I did not present the quotation of the text because I wanted to share it or felt that it should enlarge my piece here, but I had some concerns and preponderances as to the validity of some of the assertions reiterated in the text. To start with, the author asserts that blockchains are not supposed to be governed; they are supposed to be permission-less distributed ledgers, and what it is A to Z. These, to me, are an acceptance of reality in conditions in space and time and its reality being defined by stated conditions, whereby the fulfillment of the same stated conditions determines the stated reality as true and rule-bound.

I assert, contrary to the author, that blockchains are rule-bound, and their rule-boundness makes them governed and governable. Any proposition about any reality in principle is not rule-bound to me; it defies reality as we know it. Perhaps the how, who, and when of the governance may be questioned, not whether they are rule-bound. The text continues by asserting that blockchains are ecosystems with all the baggage of humans on the blockchains; otherwise, the data on their ledger has no sway in the real world. Data, be it on a centralized ledger or distributed, is generated by the ecosystem that participates in its generation to enrich or impoverish the ecosystem. As such, there is and should be a symbiosis between the data and the ecosystem; otherwise, I have some encumbrance of seeing data's existence in any ledger without any sway in the real world, as elegantly stated.

I share all the concerns of the author so far as governance, be it online or offline, as it stands, but refuse to accept that there aren't solutions or won't be for luck there of a globally thrust identity issuing authority, nor do I see the need for such an authority. Self-sovereign self-issued identity can somehow be complimented with live immutable biomarkers or DNA as complimentary to those cryptographic keys, making it impossible to clean sweep one's identity of one's past and issue and reissue oneself an identity. Perhaps one other conducive phenomenon that is very much enabling for one to jump from blockchain to blockchain and get blockchain-specific identities and be able to use them should be concerning, but blockchain interoperability is one of the greatest preoccupations of a great many in the blockchain community, which should embolden us in our assertion that one universal (global) identity tied to our immutable biomarkers won't be a mere wish but a reality in the coming. Are we there? Maybe not. Can we get there? Given all that is happening and will happen, it sure will. I am sure that the author knows that indeed, one person, one vote neither guarantees nor on itself describes democracy's existence, though one of its main manifestations, it could also lead to a dictatorship of the majority where there are minority interests and its specifically to abate such majority dictatorship that the US legislative body was divided and distributed as it is. Leaving aside all the business, professional associations, militaries, and other institutions, symbiosis and complementarity with democracies and other systems as true to the blockchains is as well true to democracy despite centuries-old democracies' existence, it is still full of fallacies and is a work in progress, and it is still far from perfect. Imperfections are so rampant in nature as they are in all man-made realities and relationships that nothing at all starts with a perfect blueprint. That as it is, I am not suggesting that blockchains are democracies or should be, but I am merely saying that every creative process and reality could and will lend lessons and help engender new progressive additions to what is.

As to democracies propagandizing, campaigning, filibustering, and forming parties, it is perhaps one of the biggest gorillas on the back of democracy. The ill that could not be done away if only there could be an alternative, but there isn't one to date. Perhaps we could find a way to propagate facts and information on time and life instead of fabricated facts and propaganda. Freedom, forks, and exits may be as easy as breaking bread in hitherto existing blockchains, but that does not necessarily mean all blockchains will do for eternity or fork and exit with impunity now, making it as painful or making exiting from nations as easy and citizenship a matter of choice rather than a matter of birthright is a long or maybe a very long strategic goal. That may not be an impossibility considering human ingenuity, the path it has traversed, and the challenges it has conquered.

In our world where only 1% of the population owns as much as what 50% of the lower-income world's population owns and where money is equated to votes, perhaps democracy and the rule of the majority is a mere mockery no less than what has thus far been said about the ineffectuality of the blockchain as a tool and mechanism for democracy to emulate. Yet no life got here by way of a squicky tidy path rather by a messy, untidy, twisty and turny path and most likely will continue forward for eternity without change, however hard an effort is made to tidy it up.

Untidyness is a permanent fixture of nature that simply can't be remedied, for tidying itself creates untidiness. The messy world we find all around us is not a creation of intentional untidiness but a byproduct of an effort to create a tidy, comfortable and liveable environment. As every human effort is constrained by the laws and ways of nature, nothing can ever be considered an effort tidy enough that it won't generate waste and unwanted debris at all but minimized and better than what is in existence in a step forward towards the long march to perfection.

Zug, a city in Switzerland known as the "Crypto Valley," has successfully completed its first test of a local blockchain-based voting system. As CoinDesk reported on June 11, the Swiss city launched an e-voting pilot platform built on a blockchain as part of the city's efforts to embrace the technology. The voting process took place between June 25 and July 1 and stored both polling information and residents' IDs on the system. SWI swissinfo.ch, a news outlet owned by the Swiss Broadcasting Corporation, reported on Monday that the city's head of communications, Dieter Müller, claimed that "the premiere was a success." Following the positive results, Müller said that "technical details" of the voting process will be evaluated over the coming months. According to a press release from the city government on June 25, the goal of building this blockchain-based platform was to make the voting process "safer and less susceptible to unnoticed manipulation." The e-voting system was developed by Luxoft, a software company based in Zug, in partnership with the city and the Department of Computer Science at the Lucerne University of Applied Sciences. At the time, Vasily Suvorov, Luxoft's chief technology officer, said: "There are concerns about electronic voting because voting is a fundamental mechanism for direct voting... That's why we believe that this technology should not belong to a single company. We will build the e-voting platform 'Open Source' so that people can understand what the technology is and how it works. We want to encourage more people to develop blockchain-based applications for governments worldwide. "Swiss flag image via Shutterstock."

Crypto Bloch chain, perhaps, is already leading the way in solving other ills of our lives before we have even been able to grasp its initial currency implementation as an asset holding distributed leger democratizing, simplifying, securing, and making monetary life of members of blockchains transparent and accountable; it is beginning to do exactly the same with politics, as is indicated in the above quotation. As this is the first and only rudimentary experiment and a successful one, it wouldn't be hard to imagine when it is perfected through trials and errors and accumulated experience that, gone will be the times of back alley money exchanges for votes, covered up illegal campaign donations for votes upon winning elective offices for not only voting but campaign ads and contributions will all be made on the blockchains where no one can hide even error corrections.

Mustafa Suleyman, in his book "The Coming Wave," argues that the world is on the cusp of a technological revolution that will have a profound impact on all aspects of our lives. He focuses on two technologies in particular: artificial intelligence (AI) and synthetic biology (SB). AI and SB are capable of transforming the world for the better, but they also pose significant risks. For example, AI could be used to create autonomous weapons that could kill without human intervention or to develop surveillance systems that could track our every move. SB could be used to create new biological weapons or to engineer new forms of life that could disrupt ecosystems. We need to start thinking now about how to mitigate the risks posed by AI and SB. He proposes a number of measures, including:

- investing in research on safety and security for AI and SB;
- Developing international treaties to regulate the development and use of these technologies;
- Educating the public about the potential benefits and risks of AI and SB. If we take these steps, we can ensure that AI and SB are used for good and not for harm. Mustafa Suleyman:

No question, the worries of the gentleman are shared and contemplated by many in government, industry, and the concerned knowledgeable of the global elite, yet humanity, like nature, solves and makes an effort to solve a problem only after the challenge becomes a barrier or a drag to forward progress, and every solution to a problem often comes with a new unforeseen challenge of its own. Above all else, the anxiety of losing control of being at the helm with every new technology that sprang up to the scene, and it can't be different this time around. Progress, by all measures, is never an end product but a beginning to what is to follow and a refinement of its progenitor. That has always been the case, and it will always be true. Every human breakthrough never passed without causing due and undue anxiety, fear, and suspicion, yet every material challenge and problem never remained a permanent, unmovable cornerstone. Every goalpost has often been moved by little and large efforts and living experiences. That being said, regulating and reaching international, national, and local treaties takes reaching a broad consensus on the perceived problem's solution far more than it could be done since the interests of the companies and industries that are working to effect and perfect both AI and SB are at times with short-term opposing and diverse interests and irreconcilable loyalties to coalesce to long-term strategic objectives.

Maybe the obsolescence of the centrally located data centers and the onset of blockchain discovery that acquisition and retention could as well serve to ease some of the worries of the author and the likes by virtue of its inherent characteristics of anonymity, mutability, and accountability of what is on the chain. The migration of data from central depositories to blockchains means that what is done in garages and back alleys, kitchens, and institutional labs would be registered on the blockchains immutably and publicly, while the data owners would remain anonymous unless deemed necessary by legal authorities in a jurisdiction or jurisdictions. Patent filings, journal publications, deed registrations, and title registrations will be done by immutable blockchain smart contracts on publicly accessible distributed ledgers. Since what is on the distributed ledger can't be altered or deleted even by the original author, designer, or composer but could only be amended with the original intact.

The need for registration or filling out with any authority is and would be unnecessary since it is and would be witnessed and time stamped prior to publication on the chain by 50+1 or more of the membership. Excuse me if I sounded and acted overly optimistic and sound like the panacea to all political ills is found, but rejoice, there is one diamond tip that could chip one sharp edge off the challenge that seems will take an eternity to find a solution for.

Works Cited

Ebrey, Patricia Buckley. Confucianism and Family Rituals in Imperial China Princeton UP, 2014. Watson, Burton. The Analects of Confucius Columbia UP, 2007. Crag, Venter (2013, October 17). Life at the Speed of Light Hachette UK. Arthur Brook, BLOCK CHAIN TECHNOLOGY AND ITS APPLICATIONS: A REVIEW. (2022, September 1). International Research Journal of Modernization in Engineering, Technology, and Science https://doi.org/10.56726/irjmets29560 Muayo Shen, Jul 2, 2018 at 21:05 UTC |

Updated Jul 3, 2018 at 11:46 UTC By Ayele Alemu Teklemariam

Abstract Summary

The paper explores the challenges of reaching a consensus in modern society and the potential of blockchain technology in promoting democracy and social justice. The author discusses factors such as relativism, individualism, and the complexity of modern life that make consensus harder to achieve. They reflect on personal experiences with democracy and dictatorship, highlighting the decline of representative democracy and the rise of minority rule. The author examines the concept of consensus in blockchain technology and its potential to address social and political issues through transparency and accountability. They express concerns about the implementation of on-chain governance, arguing for capable technologists to govern blockchains rather than democratic processes. The paper concludes by discussing different approaches to blockchain governance and mentioning a successful test of a blockchain-based voting system in Switzerland.